'Not ours, but ours to look after'

THE NATIONAL PARKS OF ENGLAND AND WALES

'Not ours, but ours to look after'

by Brian Redhead
President of the Council for National Parks
with Amanda Nobbs and Frances Rowe

PHOTOGRAPHS BY CHRIS SWAN

Oxford Illustrated Press

The Oxford Illustrated Press
© 1988, Council for National Parks and Chris Swan

ISBN 0 946609 82 9

Published by:

The Oxford Illustrated Press Limited, Haynes Publishing Group, Sparkford, Nr Yeovil, Somerset BA22 7JJ, England.

Haynes Publications Inc., 861 Lawrence Drive, Newbury Park, California 91320, USA.

Printed in England by:

J.H.Haynes & Co Limited, Sparkford, Nr Yeovil, Somerset.

British Library Cataloguing in Publication Data:

Redhead, Brian
    The National Parks of England & Wales.
    1. England. National parks
    I. Title   II. Swan, Chris
    719'.32'0942

    ISBN 0-946609-82-9

Library of Congress Catalog Card Number: 88-81061

PREFACE

This book is not a guide to the National Parks but a statement about them.

It develops and illustrates the arguments advanced in a speech delivered at the National Parks Festival, in the presence of HRH The Princess of Wales.

Its purpose is to help to make the National Parks known and understood—the better to be enjoyed.

Amanda Nobbs, the Secretary of the Council for National Parks, and Frances Rowe the Assistant Secretary, have worked with me in the preparation of this book. The proceeds from it will help to finance CNP, the National Park charity, in everything it does to protect and to promote the Parks.

Brian Redhead
President of the Council for National Parks,
45 Shelton Street, London WC2H 9HJ

For Francis Ritchie

CONTENTS

The National Parks are
the most beautiful parts
of England and Wales.
There are many other areas
of outstanding natural beauty
but none more beautiful.
That is why the National Parks
were chosen.
They are neither State-owned,
nor fenced off.
They are an inheritance,
not an invention.
And they are there to be enjoyed.

The National Park Authorities
have two principal duties:
to protect and enhance
the natural beauty of the Parks,
and to ensure that the public
has the access to enjoy them.

And if they carry out
those duties responsibly
that will ensure
the social and economic well-being
of the people who live and work
in the National Parks.

The Parks must come first.
Wherever competing interests conflict
the Parks are the priority.
And there are many threats
to their integrity.

What is quarrying
but the authorised removal of a Park?
Once you have dug out a chunk,
you cannot say that you are sorry
and that you will put it back again.
There should be no question
of quarrying in the Parks
for minerals that can be found elsewhere.

A National Park is no place
for permanent military manoeuvres,
for exercises with live ammunition,
for the requisition of beautiful acres
from which the public
is then excluded.
It is no place
for low flying military aircraft
shattering the silence of the dales.

A National Park is no place
for a tall telecommunications mast
standing out on a skyline
that needs no such decoration.

It is no place
for the planting of alien conifers
which sour the ground
and darken the landscape.
If indigenous trees will not grow
on the higher slopes,
that was what nature intended.

The Parks are there
for people to enjoy,
not for people to disfigure.
There must be access
to the open countryside,
and increasing access.

It is no place
for time share developments
which bring with them
the paraphernalia of suburbia.

But it is not enough to say
that there must be access to the Parks,
without adding access to do what?
It is one thing for walkers to ramble,
quite another for motor cyclists to scramble.
Some activities neither protect nor enhance
and they spoil everybody else's enjoyment.

It is no place
for instant villages,
or for any developer
who is inspired by greed
and whose developments
are characterised by poor taste.

To protect the National Parks
in order to enhance their beauty
is not a kill joy exercise,
a matter always of saying 'don't do that.'
It is a matter of saying:
'Don't do that, do this instead.
It will be better.'

The National Parks must be seen
not as places where
nasty things are not allowed to happen,
but as places where good things happen.

Everybody who works on the ground in the
National Parks,
will tell you what needs to be done—
what kind of farming,
what kind of building,
what kind of management—
if the Parks are to be
protected and enhanced and enjoyed.

They know that conservation,
and preservation,
and recreation,
and environment itself,
are words that can encourage
deafness not understanding.

They know that there are
too many financial incentives
to do the wrong thing
or to do nothing at all.
They know the money would be better spent
paying people to do the right things.
There is so much to do.

To look after the National Parks
is the best guarantee of livelihood
for the people in the Parks.

What is needed is for
the National Parks Authorities
to have the powers
and the money,
and the understanding,
so that they can fulfil
their obligation to their inheritance.

Future generations
will have inventions
which we cannot even dream of,
but with our help they will also have
the National Parks
that we know and love.

Dawn rising over the meadows near Challacombe, Exmoor National Park.

Hadrian's Wall in Northumberland National Park is perhaps the most famous monument to the Roman occupation of Britain.

AN INHERITANCE

*The National Parks are
the most beautiful parts
of England and Wales.
There are many other areas
of outstanding natural beauty
but none more beautiful.
That is why the National Parks
were chosen.
They are neither State-owned,
nor fenced off.
They are an inheritance,
not an invention.
And they are there to be enjoyed.*

No one invented the National Parks, they were already there. But someone had to recognise their distinction, mark them off as something special, and make sure that people could get into them.

The first ten—Northumberland, the Lake District, the Yorkshire Dales, the North York Moors, the Peak District, Snowdonia, Brecon Beacons, Pembrokeshire Coast, Dartmoor and Exmoor—all became National Parks in the 1950s, but their beauty, their tranquillity, their wildness and their solitude have been valued for centuries.

'Peace, everywhere serenity and a marvellous freedom from the tumult of the world' wrote St Aelred, abbot of Rievaulx Abbey, North Yorkshire, in the twelfth century. He was anticipating by 800 years the sentiments of a twentieth-century visitor to the North York Moors National Park, escaping the hurly-burly of city life.

More than 150 years ago, Wordsworth celebrated the beauty of the Lake District. 'I do not know any tract of country in which, in so narrow a compass may be found an equal variety in the influences of light and shadow upon the substance and beautiful features of the landscape', he wrote. He and his sister Dorothy settled in the Lakes, and Dove Cottage and Rydal Mount, their two best-known homes, are now among the most visited houses in Britain.

Wordsworth wrote one of the earliest guide books. In his *Guide to the Lakes*, he put forward the idea of the Lake District becoming 'a sort of national property, in which every man has a right and interest who has an eye to perceive and a heart to enjoy', a suggestion which would be supported, he said, 'by persons of pure taste throughout the whole island.'

It soon was. Though not perhaps by those he had in mind. Workers in the industrial towns of Victorian England were glad to escape to the countryside, and in Northern

England and the Midlands rambling became ever more popular. But most of the landowners resisted it. Freedom of the hills became a campaign by working people and in the early 1930s, gamekeepers with cudgels were still confronting walkers up on the moors. In the famous mass trespass on Kinder Scout in the Peak District, in 1932, men went to prison for daring to demand the right to ramble.

The pressure for National Parks built up both from ramblers and from countryside lovers and in 1936, the founders of the Council for National Parks—the Standing Committee for National Parks—got together to press for

Dawn clouds roll back to reveal the Vale of Edale, seen here from Mam Tor in the Peak District National Park. It was the first National Park to be designated, in 1951.

legislation. They were all there: the Ramblers' Association, the Council for the Protection (then the Preservation) of Rural England, the Friends of the Lake District, the Youth Hostels Association. These were heady times. A National Parks roadshow toured the country—the Pump Room at Bath, the Agricultural Hall in Islington. Then the war broke out, and the nation had other things on its mind.

But in 1945, National Parks became part of the plan for the reconstruction of a battered Britain. Sir Norman Birkett, a country lover and a prosecutor in the Nuremburg War Trials, recognised the change. 'It is at least inevitable that after so much sacrifice and so much suffering so nobly borne, it should be felt that some compensation might be found for so large a calamity, that something nobler should emerge for those who had endured so much, that there should be in the somewhat wistful phrase—a better world.'

National Parks were to be part of that better world. The Labour Government heeded a civil servant who was a keen rambler and a leading member of the Standing Committee. John Dower, whose son Michael is today the chief officer of the Peak Park authority, produced the definitive report on how the National Parks idea could become a reality. It was published in the same month as VE day.

It was followed by the Hobhouse Report, the report of a committee chaired by a county council chief, Sir Arthur Hobhouse, which worked out how the Parks would be run as part of local government. And in 1949 the National Parks and Access to the Countryside Act turned the National Park dream into reality. Within ten years there were ten Parks to be enjoyed. And eventually, many years later, the Norfolk and Suffolk Broads became the eleventh member of the family, a National Park in all but name.

Little Langdale, Lake District National Park

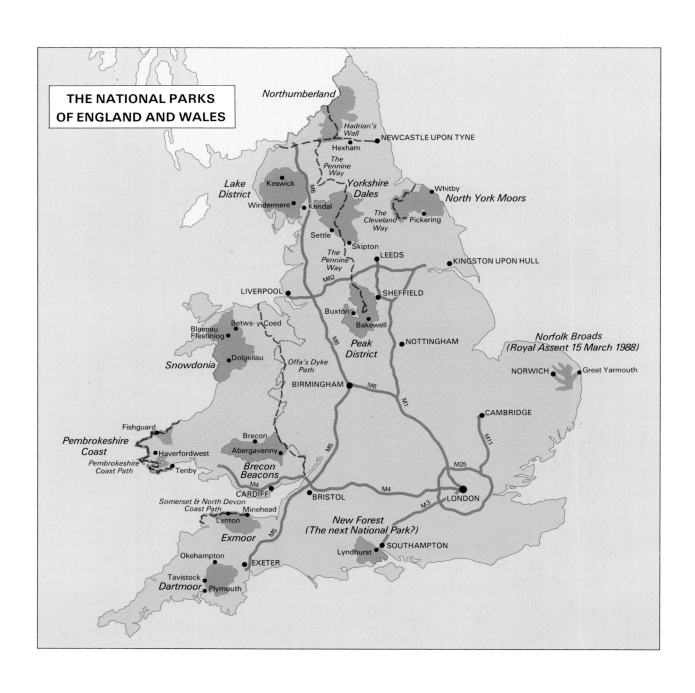

THE NATIONAL PARKS OF ENGLAND AND WALES

Northumberland

Hadrian's Wall

NEWCASTLE UPON TYNE

Hexham

The Pennine Way

Lake District

Keswick

Windermere • • Kendal

Yorkshire Dales

Whitby

North York Moors

The Cleveland Way

Pickering

Settle •

Skipton •

The Pennine Way

LEEDS

LIVERPOOL •

M62

KINGSTON UPON HULL

Blaenau Ffestiniog •

Betws-y-Coed

SHEFFIELD

Buxton •

Bakewell •

Snowdonia

Dolgellau •

Offa's Dyke Path

M6

Peak District

NOTTINGHAM •

Norfolk Broads
(Royal Assent 15 March 1988)

NORWICH • • Great Yarmouth

BIRMINGHAM •

M6

CAMBRIDGE •

Pembrokeshire Coast

Fishguard •

Brecon •

Abergavenny •

M11

Haverfordwest •

Pembrokeshire Coast Path

• Tenby

Brecon Beacons

M5

M25

M4

CARDIFF

BRISTOL •

M4

LONDON

Somerset & North Devon Coast Path

Minehead

Lynton •

M3

Exmoor

M5

New Forest
(The next National Park?)

Okehampton •

Lyndhurst • • SOUTHAMPTON

Tavistock •

Dartmoor • Plymouth

EXETER

A CELEBRATION

These next few pages celebrate the first 10 National Parks
of England and Wales, plus the Broads, which is a National
Park in all but name. Every Park is different. But all of them
should be seen not simply as scenery or background but as
wonders of creation, an experience not a setting.

PEAK DISTRICT

Pastural peacefulness at Win Hill contrasting with the drama of the moorland landscape at Higger Tor (right). Yet half an hour's drive away and you could be in Manchester or Sheffield.

Sunset over Ladybower reservoir.

THE LAKE DISTRICT

Reflections of summer in the quiet waters of Buttermere.

*Visions of Lakeland: Derwent Water at dawn
and (right) winter in Little Langdale.*

SNOWDONIA   Parc Cenedlaethol Eryri

The most northerly of the Welsh National Parks,
Snowdonia is best known for its magnificent mountain
scenery. This glorious view into the Park across Llandanwg
beach shows Mount Snowdon (3,560 ft) on the horizon.

View across Llynna Mymbyr to
Snowdon.

DARTMOOR

Dartmoor has been called southern England's last great wilderness.

More ancient stones: a medieval 'clapper' bridge—a well-known Dartmoor landmark.

The village of Lustleigh.

Hound Tor, an imposing outcrop of weathered granite rocks.

PEMBROKESHIRE COAST
Parc Cenedlaethol Penfro

The Pembrokeshire Coast National Park combines spectacular cliffs with huge golden beaches, like this one at Freshwater West.

In splendid isolation on Amroth beach.

Fishing boats at low tide, Angle Bay.

NORTH YORK MOORS

Houses sheltering from the east wind, Robin Hood's Bay.

The North York Moors National Park is an open moorland plateau intersected by hidden valleys and bordered on the east by wild and windswept cliffs. This standing stone is on Blakey Ridge, high up on the heather moorland.

The pastureland of Danby Dale.

YORKSHIRE DALES

Summer in Swaledale: haymeadows humming with insects.

The 'clints' and 'grikes' of one of the Park's characteristic limestone pavements. The snow-covered peak of Ingleborough can be seen on the skyline.

The Dales village of Dent.

Aysgarth Falls.

*The Ribblehead Viaduct, built by Victorian engineers, is
one of the splendours of the Settle Carlisle railway.*

EXMOOR

Exmoor's rolling pastures and green wooded valleys are the countryside of childhood memories.

There is nowhere more beautiful than a National Park on a spring day.

*A windswept thorn tree high up
on the moor.*

NORTHUMBERLAND

Remote and unspoilt, Northumberland National Park is beautiful and wild countryside at its finest.

The curlew is the symbol of the Park, and its plaintive cry is a familiar sound.

Hadrian's Wall is a remarkable monument to the Roman occupation of nearly 2,000 years ago.

Housesteads Fort, one of many fortifications built into the framework of the wall.

The River Coquet near Harbottle.

Corenside Common near Otterburn.

A view of the escarpment near Housesteads Fort.

BRECON BEACONS
Parc Cenedlaethol Bannau Brycheiniog

Standing stone near Ystradfellte.

The Brecon Beacons, from which the Park gets its name,
rise to the broad summit of Pen y Fan, at 2,907 ft the
highest mountain in the Park.

Crickhowel at dusk. The beautiful River Usk rises in the Park and eventually flows into the Severn Estuary at Newport.

NORFOLK BROADS

Broadland would not be the same without its windmills. They were once used to pump water from the land, but have been replaced by electric pumps.

A fishing trawler on the River Waveney heading out to the North Sea.

Halvergate grazing marshes, the first Environmentally Sensitive Area.

Eric Edwards makes his living from the Norfolk Broads by selecting and cutting reeds for thatching. It is a skilled operation. Traditional hand tools still do the best job. There is a knack to tying and stacking the bundles. It looks easy—but then that is the art of the master craftsman.

Those who campaigned long and hard for National Parks in the 1930s had a vision of unspoiled nature which could be enjoyed by everyone. One hundred years earlier, William Wordsworth put forward the Lake District as 'a sort of national property in which every man has a right and interest who has an eye to perceive and a heart to enjoy'.

THE VISION

When CNP's founders published their 'Case for National Parks in Great Britain' in 1938, the foreword to the document was by the most famous historian in England at that time, G M Trevelyan. He wrote these words.

'The Government undertakes to assist the health of the nation and to find playing fields for the dwellers in the vast cities to play cricket and football. But it is no less essential, for any national health scheme, to preserve for the nation walking grounds and regions where young and old can enjoy the sight of unspoiled nature.

'And it is not a question of physical exercise only, it is also a question of spiritual exercise and enjoyment. It is a question of spiritual values. Without sight of the beauty of nature the spiritual power of the British people will be atrophied.'

He was right. Beautiful countryside makes you feel good. It cheers you up. You go for a walk in the hills and the world seems a better place. Even if you do not go there, it is reassuring to know that in this overcrowded island there is somewhere unspoilt. National Parks are good for the soul.

The Standing Committee in 1938 said this about the desirability of National Parks:

'Great Britain has a strictly limited amount of unspoilt wilder country and there are many encroachments upon it—not only for weekend cottages, new or improved motor roads, car-parks, filling-stations, road-houses, advertisement hoardings and all the paraphernalia that meet the needs of the "country lover", but also for such economic and public developments as water-catchment, electric power schemes, artillery and bombing grounds, mining, quarrying and commercial afforestation.

'There is not a square mile too much of wilder country, and there is urgent need of a national policy for conserving the whole.'

They were right. They wanted beautiful and wild landscapes to be protected and made available for public enjoyment, and open-air recreation and traditional farming preserved. And with the passing of the 1949 Act they believed it had all come true.

'There is not a square mile too much of wilder country,
and there is urgent need of a national policy for
conserving the whole'—Standing Committee on
National Parks, 1938.

Our Parks are the result of the handiwork of men and women over the centuries. This attractive 'patchwork quilt' arrangement of small fields and stone walls in the Yorkshire Dales has been shaped by farmers tending the land.

THE VISION
CLOUDED

*The National Park Authorities
have two principal duties:
to protect and enhance the natural beauty of the Parks,
and to ensure that the public
has the access to enjoy them.*

*And if they carry out
those duties responsibly
that will ensure the social and economic well-being
of the people who live and work
in the National Parks.*

National Parks are not what they should be. They have never been allowed to do a proper job. But even though they have been denied power and money for nearly forty years, they have given pleasure to more people than anyone ever dreamed of.

The National Parks were never intended to be empty wilderness. They are places where people live and work, and they owe much to the handiwork of men and women over centuries. As John Dower said in his original report: 'The landscape to be preserved is the joint product of nature and of human use over many generations; it cannot be preserved in anything like its present aspect unless that human use is kept fully going.'

To ensure local involvement in something of national importance, his idea was for each National Park to be run by an authority comprised of two-thirds local councillors and one-third people chosen by the government because of their particular knowledge and experience. Like the local councils in the rest of the country, these National Park Authorities would be able to grant or refuse planning permission to would-be developers.

The Town and Country Planning Act of 1947 had given the councils planning powers for the first time. It was all part of the post-war building of a better Britain: deliberately choosing how the country should look rather than the pre-War free-for-all which had brought 'ribbon' development—straggles of unchecked building, often alongside main roads—and a 'pink rash' of bungalows spreading over England.

The Peak Park was the first National Park to be set up. That was in 1951. Because there were six county councils in the Park, an independent 'joint board' was formed to run the Park, with representatives from each of the councils. As a Board from the word go, the Park had its own boss, its own staff, and the power to raise its own money. The Lake District followed the same year, but it had no separate staff to run it.

By the time the tenth National Park, the Brecon Beacons, was designated in 1957, things had gone seriously wrong. The county councils were guarding their new planning powers and they were not going to surrender them to the National Parks without a fight. In the end, the remaining eight Parks were run merely as county council committees, like social services committees or education committees, but of no special interest to most of the councillors who served on them. Unlike the Boards, Park Committees lacked independence and clout.

In the early 1960s Britain, according to the Prime

The vision clouded: National Parks had no sooner been set up than governments were seeking to undermine them. In the late 1950s a nuclear power station went ahead in Snowdonia, and Hinkley B, another of the early Magnox reactors (right), was built just outside Exmoor National Park.

Minister, Harold Macmillan, had 'never had it so good'. The economy was booming and families were better off. For the first time people could afford a car, a television, a refrigerator. Motorways, power stations, reservoirs were built. With the austerity of war time still in recent memory, the late '50s and early '60s were a time of having more and enjoying it unashamedly. The National Parks 'shared' in the general prosperity but in a way which horrified the campaigners of the 1930s.

A huge oil refinery was constructed at Milford Haven, in the Pembrokeshire Coast National Park. The Trawsfynnydd nuclear power station went ahead in Snowdonia and one of the most famous planners of the time actually said 'no national park is really complete without a nuclear power station'. New reservoirs drowned valleys, quarries defaced hillsides. Power lines criss-crossed in all directions. And private cars poured into the Parks. Even pop festivals were a problem according to the Standing Committee for National Parks.

The National Parks did not seem to mean much to anyone, certainly not to Government departments. And local councils were more interested in bringing new jobs to their areas than in worrying about the National Parks they were meant to be protecting.

The Government's response to criticism of what was going on in the National Parks was an Act of Parliament in 1968 which imposed a feeble duty over all public bodies to 'have regard to the desirability of conserving the natural beauty and amenity of the countryside'. Weak words which meant that on the ground nothing really changed.

In the early 1970s the Government set out to reform local government but achieved only reorganisation. Overnight Rutland disappeared off the map and many people woke up in different counties.

In the Pembrokeshire Coast National Park an oil refinery was constructed at Milford Haven.

Quarrying for slate at Elterwater in the Lake District.

This seemed the moment to do something about the National Parks: they certainly needed it. The Standing Committee (now the Council for National Parks) pressed for all the Parks to be run by independent boards, like the Peak Park. But the county councils resisted. The final compromise in 1972 was that the Parks would be run as single united authorities, with their own staff and chief officer. But the Peak and the Lakes remained the only Parks with independent boards. For the first time, the National Parks were to plan how they would protect and enhance the Parks and provide for people's enjoyment.

Since 1949 the National Parks had all been financed through the rates with the Government chipping in for such items as car parks and toilets. But the Local Government Act of 1974 provided for a special grant from the Government of 75 per cent of the costs of running the Parks, with the county councils making up the remaining 25 per cent.

The most far-reaching developments in the countryside, and those which have brought about the biggest changes to the National Parks are in the industries over which the Parks have no real powers: farming and forestry.

And with planning rules being relaxed throughout the countryside, the National Parks could face a depressing future as damaging and irrevocable developments are allowed by government.

It all sounds gloomy, but it need not be. Much has been achieved in the Parks in spite of all the difficulties. Much more can be achieved. The Parks are still only tinkering with the work which needs to be done. There can be more good things in these beautiful places.

Walkers enjoying a stroll where Tarr Steps, an unusual stepped clapper bridge, crosses the River Beale at Dulverton, Exmoor. All the National Parks run a programme of guided walks where visitors can find out more about the history of the local landscape.

FOR PEOPLE TO ENJOY

*The Parks are there
for people to enjoy,
not for people to disfigure.
There must be access
to the open countryside,
and increasing access.*

*But it is not enough to say
that there must be access to the Parks,
without adding access to do what?
It is one thing for walkers to ramble,
quite another for motor cyclists to scramble.
Some activities neither protect nor enhance
and they spoil everybody else's enjoyment.*

National Parks are there to be enjoyed. And there are many ways of enjoying them: walking, climbing, sailing, riding or just admiring the view.

Britain's National Parks are national but they are not nationalised: not all land in the National Parks is open to the public. It all depends on who the landlord is. The National Trust, which owns nearly a tenth of the Lake District, allows people to roam freely over its land. The Forestry Commission, which is the government agency in charge of the nation's tree growing, has a policy of allowing people in its forests. And although the National Park Authorities themselves cannot afford to buy much land, what they do own is freely available for public enjoyment.

But the Ministry of Defence and some of those who like hunting, shooting and fishing place their land out of bounds. Even public bodies which own land in the Parks exclude the public. Some water authorities still claim that walkers would pollute water supplies if allowed near reservoirs, although in recent years a few of them have changed their minds.

Walking is now the most popular outdoor recreation in Britain—11 million people regularly pull on their walking boots and few of them could resist a splendid 'ridge' such as this. Unfortunately, path erosion is now a problem in all of the National Parks. In the Brecon Beacons a muddy smear marks the main path up Pen Y Fan. If there were a 'right to roam' across all hills and mountains, the load would be spread and erosion much reduced. Such a right still does not exist in law.

The Park Authorities do a lot to ensure that people enjoy the Parks. They have done a very good job turning some of the simpler walks into interesting excursions. In the spring people may visit seabird colonies on the islands of the Pembrokeshire Coast National Park, or take the children mammal tracking, or go on a coastal ramble to enjoy the wild flowers. In Northumberland people can discover the life of a pond, or the wildlife of the night, or join a 'hunt' for the wild mountain goat. Winter in Snowdonia offers the chance to learn some Welsh history, traditional crafts, plus walks in the mountains to get over the excesses of Christmas. All the Parks have first-class information centres.

To move on from the guided walks and the well-known routes, to the lesser-known footpaths of the National Parks is exhilarating. But it can be frustrating. Barbed wire or a padlock may bar the way—on a footpath—although this is strictly illegal. In summer, paths are often overgrown and impenetrable—although farmers have a duty to keep them unobstructed. Signs are frequently missing.

If an afternoon stroll has turned out to be too eventful, the would-be adventurer thinks twice before trying new routes again.

The problem is that the Park Authorities simply do not have the money to keep the footpath network intact, or the time to take the few awkward landowners to task. The Peak District, the Brecon Beacons, most of Snowdonia and part of the North York Moors do not even have the powers to look after their own foothpaths—in those Parks the county councils are still in charge of public rights of way.

And yet some Park Authorities have made a little money go a long way and have also taken advantage of oppor- tunities for creating new footpaths. In the Peak Park, the Tissington Trail for walkers and cyclists has replaced a disused railway with a much-used path.

Footpaths make good sense to the people whose livelihood depends on the Parks. Walkers need feeding, watering, and somewhere to stay, and the money they spend on themselves and their families means money for local communities providing those services. Many farmers recognise this—and far from resenting visitors welcome walkers. Money spent on footpaths by National Parks is an investment which benefits whole communities.

The Park authorities need to be alert to the danger of overinterpreting the National Parks. Not every walker wants to be led by the hand. Signs all over the open moors would look very silly. Wild countryside is in short supply and we should not try to tame it too much. In remoter areas, discreet signs marking the way and simple cutting back of undergrowth on paths once a year is all that is needed. With a basic knowledge of map and compass—and there are many outdoor organisations willing to teach it—the National Parks should be open country in every sense.

There are some magnificent long-distance paths in the Parks—the Pennine Way which passes through the Peak District, the Yorkshire Dales and Northumberland, and the Pembrokeshire Coast Path which extends for more than 184 miles along the Welsh coastline. These paths are particularly popular because obstructions, whether deliberate or resulting from neglect, are very few. Walkers are virtually guaranteed hours of happy walking whether they choose to walk a few miles, or the whole distance. Paradoxically, that is exactly why parts of the Pennine Way are more like a pedestrianised motorway than a footpath. It is all those feet treading the same well-known path.

In the Yorkshire Dales, the Three Peaks—Ingleborough, Penyghent and Whernside—are said to be suffering from

Twisted tree on Rushup Edge in the Peak Park with the unstable peak of Mam Tor in the background.

the worst erosion in Britain. Many of the paths to the summit are now twice the width of a B class road: more than 200,000 people climb the Peaks each year. An annual challenge walk and a cyclo-cross race have not helped.

There is a special committee of the Yorkshire Dales National Parks tackling the problem. The total repair bill could be well over £1 million.

Fishing on Wimbleball Lake, Exmoor National Park.

A joy to behold is Jacob's Ladder at the southern end of the Pennine Way, owned by the National Trust, where the crumbling footpath which had suffered from years of heavy foot traffic, has been replaced by stone steps which look as if they have been there since the Iron Age. The young men and women on the government work scheme who did the repairs used Iron Age engineering techniques too, so it should last for a few thousand years at least. It just shows what can be done.

If all those feet are not to tread the same well worn path, what is to be done? Forty years ago, John Dower, and the other members of the Standing Committee for National Parks, wanted everyone to have the legal right to roam where they wanted over all uncultivated or 'open' countryside—moors and mountains, rough hillside pastures, heaths, commons, lakesides, riversides and the coast—while using the public footpaths and bridleways to travel across farmland.

But their ideas were severely diluted by the 1949 Act—no doubt because of pressure from landowners—and today there is still no legal right to roam across open country. National Park Authorities can negotiate special agreements with landowners to allow people to walk across their land or can impose compulsory 'access orders'. But, with the exception of the Peak Park—which now has agreements with landowners to allow the public over much of the land where the ramblers and gamekeepers clashed in the 1930s—the Parks have been shy of making agreements or orders and wary of having to pay the compensation bill. But should taxpayers' money 'reward' landowners for granting rights of passage? Should not there be a right of access to moors and mountains?

The Parks have a wealth of wildlife and occasionally this creates a conflict of interests between walkers and nature-lovers. Although there is little evidence to suggest that

National Park rangers Gail Griffith (left) and Gary Bacon (right) hard at work helping the public to find their way around the Peak District National Park. The rangers are the essential people on the ground who ensure that the Parks are looked after and enjoyed.

walkers unsettle shy animals and birds, most people are quite happy to agree to temporary restrictions on their freedom where rare birds are nesting, or where fragile plants grow.

There has been much hot air and rhetoric expended on the subject of walkers and grouse, but researchers at the Game Conservancy have found that grouse are not disturbed by walkers provided they do not have dogs with them. Grouse also do not seem to be too worried by bombs and shells on the army ranges in Northumberland or by proximity to railway lines, or to quarry blasting! (Perhaps they are just bird-brained). The rule seems to be that constant disturbance is tolerated but spasmodic and non-routine interference ruffles their feathers, so everyone should avoid erratic intrusion into their privacy.

There is a National Park 'rule' which says that conservation should come before public enjoyment if there is a conflict, but striking a balance between wildlife and people is better. Sometimes the two can help each other. In an attempt to prevent robbers stealing eggs from the nests of the rare Goshawk, the Royal Society for the Protection of Birds wants to have public hides in the Peak District which will allow people to view the birds, and enable them to act as lookouts for spotting the thieves.

More than 90 million people a year visit the National Parks. That is a lot of people. There is only one way of being sure that the National Parks can stand up to the pressure of being so popular and that is to put them first. If they are to be protected and enhanced it may be necessary at times for ramblers to take a different path up the mountain or for drivers to leave their cars behind in the car park or for motorcyclists who choose to disfigure the mountainsides to ride elsewhere.

Enjoying a little nostalgia . . . From spring to late autumn the platform at Grosmont Station in the North York Moors is crowded with people waiting for the steam train to take them through Newtondale. Trains run throughout the year. Steam buffs have been known to hold their wedding receptions on the move in the restored restaurant cars.

Bakewell cattle market in the Peak District at first light. Hill farmers keep hardy breeds of sheep which are able to withstand the cold of winter and which can survive on the meagre hill grazings. The farmers hope their ewes will produce a lamb each year. The lambs run with their mothers until the autumn. Then they are sold at the markets to be fattened on lowland farms where the grazing is better quality.

THE ESSENTIAL INHABITANTS

*Everybody who works on the ground in the
National Parks,
will tell you what needs to be done—
what kind of farming,
what kind of building,
what kind of management—
if the Parks are to be
protected and enhanced and enjoyed.*

*They know that there are
too many financial incentives
to do the wrong thing
or to do nothing at all.
They know that the money would be better spent
paying people to do the right things.
There is so much to do.*

*To look after the National Parks
is the best guarantee of livelihood
for the people in the Parks.*

Farmers are the essential inhabitants of the National Parks. Without them there would be no Parks. It was they who shaped the landscapes that we love, although they did sometimes overdo it. John Dower himself, in his original report, recognised the importance of farming in the National Parks.

'It is above all else to farming, both to the extensive grazing of the higher open land and to the more or less intensive grazing, mowing and cropping of the lower, fully enclosed land, that the landscapes of all our potential National Parks owe the man-made element in their character; and it is to the farming communities that we must look for continuance not only of the scenic setting but of the drama itself—the rural life and work, "the mild continuous epic of the soil", the endless battle between man and nature—without which the finest of English or Welsh scenery would lack an essential part of its charm and recreational value.'

Farming has shaped the National Park landscapes more than any other activity. For centuries, sheep farmers like James Atkinson have tended their flocks on the hills. Without the sheep, there would be no heather moorland—trees would have taken over long ago. It is important that traditional farming is maintained, both for the beauty of the Parks and the survival of local communities. It would be sad if the Parks were simply on show to visitors.

And that is no less true now. One of the best things about the National Parks is the farmed landscape in the valleys and dales. Tiny fields of a multiplicity of greens, packed neatly into pockets of land. In the Dales or the White Peak the borders and boundaries are formed by miles of dry stone walls made from local limestone, wonderful creations which withstand the foulest weather. From afar they form a maze of pattern. The Dales are studded with barns made from the natural stone and the countryside would not be the same without them. Up on the moors, the grazing of sheep keeps the heather short and springy; if there were no sheep, the land would quickly revert to bushes and scrubby woodland.

Traditional farming has therefore shaped the Parks and those 'traditional' landscapes have proved remarkably resilient. The countryside in the National Parks is still lovely. But the damage which has afflicted the wider countryside over the last thirty, and particularly the last fifteen, years, has not left the Parks untouched.

Neither Dower, nor the architects of the 1949 Act could have foreseen the technological revolution which was to take place in agriculture, nor the government policies which were to spur farmers on to greater and greater production at the expense of the countryside. They did not believe that the farming and forestry industries were in any way threatening to the Parks: indeed Dower said 'farming could and should be greatly improved in most National Park areas ... Such improvement is in no way inconsistent with the landscape preservation and recreational requirements of a National Park regime.' He was wrong, but he was not to know. He was writing at the end of the Second World War when the engine of agricultural production was only just warming up. He died in 1947 before any of the dangers were obvious and sadly

Blakey Ridge, North York Moors. Subsidies and grants to farmers, coupled with modern farming techniques, have encouraged the draining of the moors and their reseeding with grass. In the North York Moors, 5000 hectares (13,000 acres) of beautiful heather moorland has been lost since the war.

before he was able to see his beloved Parks come into being.

Since then we have all seen hedges ripped up to accommodate machinery; chemicals applied to the land in ever-increasing amounts; the loss of many of our wild flowers. In the Yorkshire Dales hay meadows full of flowers have been ploughed, drained and fertilised. Large numbers of sheep have overgrazed the hills and mountains in Snowdonia and the Lake District. Moorland has been converted into pasture on the North York Moors, on Dartmoor, and on Exmoor, where the mild climate and gentler terrain have encouraged the losses. Dry stone walls and hedges have been replaced by post and wire fences in all the Parks, and fencing of the open fells is a growing menace.

Walls and fences. If dry stone walls are not maintained they soon fall into disrepair and are replaced with post and wire. Here in the Brecon Beacons as in the other Parks, fencing across the open fells is a growing problem. Some Parks are now running schemes to help farmers to look after their walls.

The very farming landscapes we treasure have been disappearing at an alarming rate because, since the war, all governments have been anxious to secure food supplies. They have encouraged home production by a massive injection of grants and subsidies to farmers. At the same time, fertiliser and chemicals have increased the farmers' ability to produce more food from the same acreage. Farmers could not go wrong: the more they grew, the more they were paid and the richer they became. Or at least some of them did.

When Britain joined the EEC in 1973, even more money was pumped into the system. What consumers did not realise was that their money was being given to farmers to destroy the countryside in the name of self-sufficiency. What farmers and successive governments failed to realise was that the national appetite was changing. Along with the rest of the EEC, we began producing more food than we needed. By the time anybody important noticed, the cost of growing the surplus food and then getting rid of it again was threatening to bankrupt the system. And what everyone took a long time to notice was that we were looking after food production at the expense of looking after farmers.

Large farmers were better able to exploit the grants and subsidies: they were more eligible—the smallest and part time farmers did not even qualify for payments. Large farmers had more money to begin with, which made it easier to attract larger grants, and they had more acres on which to produce more food for which they then received more subsidies. The bigger farmers became bigger while the smaller ones could not compete and went out of business. Everywhere, machines replaced men on the land.

In the National Parks, on the inhospitable uplands where farming has always been a battle with the elements, small

family farms have gone to the wall because of the folly of farming policies. Farming jobs have been lost—to the detriment of rural communities. In Northumberland where the high moors and hills between Hadrian's wall and the Cheviots are difficult farming country, the number of full-time jobs dropped from 935 in 1951 to 300 in 1980.

National Park farmers, caught like everyone else in the intensification trap, invested in producing more beef and sheep. With grants, they drained their meadows, changed from hay to silage, converted their moorland, increased their stocking rates, built farm roads and new buildings for their animals. Many borrowed from the banks to do this.

The government's response in 1981, when it seemed the situation was getting dangerously out of hand, was to introduce a silly system for paying farmers 'compensation' for agreeing not to damage the environment. This compensation was to be linked to what the farmer could have earned if he had used the publicly funded grants on offer to 'improve' his land, to produce more food nobody wanted, at the expense of the environment everyone cherished.

Sheep grazing among the trees beside the still waters of Wimbleball Lake, Exmoor National Park. Grazing animals nibble away the layers of small shrubs and seedling trees which develop naturally in woodlands, leaving behind gappy trees known as 'wood pasture'. It is important to get the balance right between animals and trees. Woods which are overgrazed will not regenerate and will eventually die. So it may be necessary to fence out the animals temporarily until the young trees are tall enough to be safe from predatory teeth.

In National Parks, farmers have to inform the Park Authorities when they apply to the Ministry of Agriculture for a grant. The Park Authorities can recommend refusal if they think the countryside is at risk. They then have to offer the farmer a 'management agreement' at enormous cost. In 1985 the Government was more inspired and in National Parks introduced new controls over farm buildings and roads, many of which had already snaked their way surreptitiously over miles of hillsides.

Obviously no system which relies on a form of bribery can survive for long; there is not the money to sustain it, and while farmers are encouraged to go on producing more, it can never work. Clearly, there should be a different kind of farming, a different set of farming priorities.

One fact remains the same: there must be farmers in National Parks. The traditional landscapes depend on them. And the way to keep them there is by encouraging the right kind of farming, the kind which protects and enhances the National Parks, which benefits farm incomes, which brings tourists, which benefits local communities, and which allows greater public freedom of the Parks. Taxpayers' money would be much better spent on this.

The right things are now beginning to happen. The Environmentally Sensitive Areas experiment, in which National Parks are playing an important part, is a deliberate attempt to protect the most beautiful and fragile countryside, together with its buildings and history, with the full involvement of farmers. The Government has singled out certain areas of the country to be Environmentally Sensitive Areas, where farmers are being paid to farm in sympathy with their environment. In the Yorkshire Dales ESA, where so many flower-rich hay meadows are threatened because of modern farming practices, and many traditional farm buildings and boundaries are in ruins, farmers can enter a scheme whereby they are paid to nurture their meadows through low-intensity farming, (no chemicals and gentler grazing) and to maintain their dry stone walls and barns, using natural materials.

In the North Peak ESA in the Peak District, farmers are being paid to look after their heather moorland—which is an important home for grouse and other birds—and to protect other fragile areas through traditional farming methods.

Some National Parks are funding their own experiments. In Dartmoor, the Park Authority gives farmers grants towards the upkeep of their ancient beech hedgerows, and the result is a delight, and a fine home for birds and wild flowers.

In the North York Moors and Exmoor, farm advisers are seeing whether they can return grassland, converted in the cause of maximum food production, back to moorland.

Two kinds of farming near Widecombe in the Moor, Dartmoor. On the right undrained pasture, home to a rich variety of wildlife and left, the same sort of pasture drained and reseeded.

Farm buildings in Northumberland. The modern all purpose building on the right, paid for largely by the taxpayer, could be anywhere in the country.

This has especial relevance as land comes out of food production. Now is the time to make good the damage, to encourage the return of wildlife, even to enhance the appearance of the landscape. The pioneering work taking place in National Parks will have valuable lessons for the rest of the countryside. Perhaps one day, when farmers in the Dales have succeeded in restoring beautiful meadows, their knowledge and experience can teach others.

However, it is important that farmers farm, and do not feel that they are simply glorified Park keepers. They have pride in their farming knowledge and expertise. The new environmentally-aware farming combines traditional methods with the up-to-date. It revives skills and crafts. It creates jobs. It is good both for farmers and for farming, and the government should encourage it. At the same time any grants which help to bring the new farming about must be structured so that, while the countryside and the public benefit, farmers feel in charge of their farms, making decisions based on their own judgement, as they have always done.

Visitors are crucial to the survival of many Park dwellers, including farmers, some of whom are diversifying into new activities, such as farm shops, or holiday cottages. Some farmers are converting redundant barns into low cost accommodation for walkers. By providing greater public access to their land, such as farm trails or new footpaths, or better management of the old ones, they are guaranteed a steady supply of customers the year round.

Farmers in National Parks increasingly know that by investing in people's enjoyment by giving them access makes sound sense, that taking care of the National Parks is good for their pockets and for everyone elses'. Almost alone they can argue that the Parks are both theirs and theirs to look after.

Traditional farm buildings have a strong regional identity and help to make a landscape beautiful.

Hedgerows and woodland make a landscape: what would the National Parks be without trees?

RETURN OF THE NATIVES

A National Park
is no place
for the planting of alien conifers
which sour the ground
and darken the landscape.
If indigenous trees will not grow
on the higher slopes,
that was what nature intended.

Old Burtness Wood stands above the green strip of land which separates Crummock Water from Buttermere in the north west corner of the Lake District. Gnarled and stubby oak trees, birch and mountain ash trees hang precariously on the steep slopes. These are wonderful woods, festooned with delicate lacy lichens and ferns, where squelchy mosses of a hundred different greens form the forest floor and grow over the rocks and stones.

Such ancient woodlands are magical places, the stuff of fairy tales and folklore. Friendly places too which once provided the farmer with fuel and building materials, and were the foraging grounds for his animals. Rural communities relied on these woodlands.

New Burtness Wood, next door to Old Burtness Wood, is jam packed with straight trunked conifer species from abroad, lined up in regimental rows. Aliens such as sitka spruce have marched their way across many of the most beautiful parts of the National Parks, in Northumberland, in the Brecon Beacons. They are unfriendly. Their shadow is dark, their forest floor soured and uninviting. They destroy open moorland which provides nesting sites for the more finicky birds. And when the wind blows, many of the trees fall down.

The National Trust, which owns both Burtness Woods, knows that in a National Park, the ancient natural forests are much to be preferred. They are an irreplaceable part of the Parks, of inestimable value, for wildlife and for peoples' enjoyment, and for the beauty of the landscape. So it is gradually substituting for New Burtness Wood a baby Old Burtness Wood, as an investment for generations to come.

In the National Parks, there are still many natural woodlands to enjoy—in Exmoor, in Northumberland, in Snowdonia—but they need special care if they are to survive.

A graceful avenue of trees in Birchcleave wood near Simonsbath. Oak predominates in Exmoor's remaining deciduous woodlands. Many were coppiced up until the early part of this century.

The march of the conifer must be halted. This march began in the 1930s, when the Forestry Commission, the government's forestry agency, began planting conifer forests all over the place to boost home-grown timber production. Ennerdale in the Lake District is one of its forests.

Then a city tax avoider calculated that if rich people invested their money in trees, they could save themselves a lot of tax. Soon many people were doing it. Forestry companies which were hired by investors to look after the forests also grew rich. Investors in forests could claim grant from the Forestry Commission to plant their trees. With tax incentives and grants they could not lose. Consequently the march of aliens accelerated, particularly in the uplands, where land is cheaper and conifers grow faster and produce a cash crop of timber faster than other trees.

But the money the trees yield does not go into local pockets. Farmers have been persuaded to sell their land to forestry companies; while any jobs the alien forests create are for gangs of contract labour, who always move on.

Tax handouts to desecrate the countryside became an embarrassment to some and an outrage to others. In the 1988 budget, the Government put a stop to tax-fuelled forestry. The Environment Minister said that large conifer forests on the English hills would no longer be allowed. Sadly, no such protection was given to Wales or Scotland.

But days later the grants for planting trees were increased dramatically as part of an equation carefully calculated to compensate for the loss of tax incentives for tree planting. Tax savings had been replaced with larger planting grants. In the words of a leading forester, 'If I had a lot of money, I would still be interested in planting trees'. But will they be of the right kind and in the right places?

Cam Fell in the north west of the Yorkshire Dales, where farmland is under threat from afforestation. The open landscape would be dramatically altered if planting were to go ahead.

The geometric uniformity of a conifer plantation in Redesdale, Northumberland.

Government tells us that a new mood has emerged. The grants for planting on 'improved' land—rather than on moorland—are higher. Farmers are to be encouraged to plant for themselves rather than being squeezed out by the forestry companies. The grants for planting deciduous trees have been increased by over 150 per cent. But the grants for planting conifers have been increased by over 250 per cent. Conifers are still an attractive option.

Business-like ranks of young trees on a commercial
plantation at Y Gelli in the Brecon Beacons. As the
trees mature they close ranks to form a dark,
impenetrable wall, of little use to the wildlife they have
displaced.

Whether Government promises will result in woodland we can be proud of, or turn out to be little more than window dressing, is yet to be seen. The rewards for planting trees are higher than they have ever been. There is all to play for.

The ancient forests should be recognised and valued for what they are: not commercial timber plantations, but beautiful places for wildlife and people. That would be a sensible and sensitive use of subsidy. Farmers and landowners should be paid to look after them. In the past, grazing animals in woodlands was a common practice, but an absence of shepherding has left the woodlands badly overgrazed. The sheep eat the baby trees and the woods are not renewed. Landowners need help to put up fences to keep stock out, for a temporary period, until the baby trees are out of danger. And they need help to revive the art of shepherding. There is nothing to beat one man and a good dog.

And farmers must be encouraged to use their woods again. Woods which are used wisely will last forever. A hundred years ago, clumps of trees were regularly felled every five to fifteen years or so, and then they grew again from the trunk in fine straight poles, designed by nature to be useful. There are many rural crafts which could make good use of this wood and provide an income for the farmers. And then perhaps the wooden furniture in all the smart shops will not be made from ash, oak and beech which has been imported, but will be fashioned by home-grown craftsmen using home-grown wood.

The National Parks themselves should have control over forestry, so that large (or small) ugly plantations do not in future disfigure the Parks. They need full planning controls so that they can determine the size of any new forests, where they are to be planted, and what type of trees are

A farmhouse fringed by a horseshoe of conifers in the Yorkshire Dales. Farmers are being encouraged to plant trees on their land.

We lumberjacks three. Peak Park foresters Dave Standen, Pete Enion and Dave Goodwin take a break from work. National Parks are becoming increasingly involved in looking after woodland.

to be planted. And this control should cover the new woodlands which the government is encouraging farmers to plant on their land.

The National Parks require special powers to prevent landowners going ahead with new forests against everyone else's wishes. And above all, they need the staff to help farmers to plant woodlands that will enrich the National Parks.

The uniform dark green of the plantation contrasts with the variety of hues in the surrounding moors and hills of the Cheviots.

*Native Scots pine at the head of Crummock Water, in the
Lake District.*

Stone circle on Dartmoor. The purpose of such prehistoric monuments can only be guessed at, but historians believe they had considerable religious significance.

A LEGACY IN STONE

National Parks are not unoccupied open spaces. They have been people's homes for centuries; this is where they lived and worked and their occupation has left its monuments. Some are humble and ordinary, like gate posts and barns. Some are grand and extravagant, like castles and cathedrals. Some are of exceeding antiquity, like stone circles and standing stones. Some are more recent and industrial like mills and kilns. But all are a reminder that wherever you go in a National Park, someone has been there before. And the good things left behind are as worthy of protection as the landscape itself. In preserving and protecting the buildings in the National Parks we are hanging on to our history.

*The Dales village of Askrigg, known to millions as
Darrowby, the home of television vet James Herriott.*

Every National Park has treasures which are entirely its own and all the more special because of it. Northumberland National Park has a wonderfully rich inheritance of 'bastle barns', fortified barns built in the days of cross-border thieving and raids. Dartmoor has the standing stones of immeasurable age, such as Beardown Man, the Bronze Age huts of Walkman Valley, the medieval Clapper Bridges—huge slabs of granite on stone piers, built so well that some are still standing today; the Dartmoor 'long-houses'—which accommodated people and animals in one long building from the fourteenth to the seventeenth century. Many survive, although they have been altered. The longhouse of Higher Uppacott was purchased by the Dartmoor National Park in 1978 to preserve it intact.

The Pembrokeshire Coast National Park has the magnificent cathedral of St Davids in the 'village' of the same name, (it is in fact Britain's smallest city). The North York Moors has fine monasteries and abbeys, of which Rievaulx Abbey in Ryedale is perhaps the best known.

The Welsh National Parks have many fine castles: Carreg Cennen Castle in the Brecon Beacons, Castell Dolwyddelan in Snowdonia. Would castles get planning permission today? Would Chatsworth House in the Peak District?

Protection for buildings in the National Parks varies greatly. At the top end of the scale of protection, are listed buildings: Grade I, of national importance; Grade II, of regional or local importance. Grade I buildings are entitled to grants towards their upkeep from government agencies. The money to look after Grade II buildings has to come largely from the Parks' themselves and the amounts they have available to spend come nowhere near to meeting the costs. The Parks have around 15,000 listed buildings between them, but can only tap into government money if these are in special 'conservation areas'. It is ironic that conservation areas should be needed at all in National Parks!

Lowlier buildings—the more commonplace or every-day, rely on loving owners and on remaining useful. Without doubt, the most effective way of preserving all traditional buildings in the National Parks, listed or other-wise, is to find a new use for them. Once a building becomes redundant, its future is inevitably uncertain. Redundancy and dereliction are the first steps on the road to demolition.

Barns which have fallen into disuse are the frequent casualties of modern farming methods. In the Yorkshire Dales, the limestone barns in the valleys are a much treasured part of the countryside, but as hay-making has declined and machinery has become too large for its traditional quarters, many barns have become tumbling ruins, too expensive for farmers to keep for aesthetic reasons alone. In the Peak District, too, barns have fallen into disuse.

These dry stone walls and a field barn, made from local limestone, are a much loved feature of the 'White Peak' in the Peak Park. But their future is uncertain. Modern farming methods have made many of them redundant and their upkeep can be expensive, in terms of both materials and manpower. The Yorkshire Dales has launched a scheme to pay local farmers to conserve the Park's dry stone walls and an estimated 10,000 barns.

A perfect match. These farm buildings at Rushup Edge in the Peak Park blend in perfectly with their surroundings. They are as much a part of the view as the trees, flowers and fields.

But both Parks experimented with schemes to grant-aid farmers to convert their barns into simple accommodation for walkers—'bunkhouse barns' in the Yorkshire Dales, and the simpler 'stone tents' in the Peak. The Countryside Commission has now introduced a national scheme which in addition to helping farmers in the National Parks to retain their traditional farm buildings, will enrich the whole countryside.

The character of whole villages is shaped by the buildings. In the Peak park village of Longnor, in North-East Staffordshire, the market hall, where farmers once met face to face to haggle over prices, gradually became redundant as telephone trading took over. A few years ago, the building stood empty. Then in 1983 a special experiment run by the Park for revitalising rural communities enabled the market hall to be converted into a craft workshop, creating local jobs. As part of the same scheme, in the village of Monyash, an old barn was converted into a plumbers' workshop and a self-catering holiday flat.

In these days of mass production, National Parks still have a welcome individuality. Small details of a porch or doorway stamp an indelible regional identity on a building.

The Lake District National Park is putting together a scheme for the lasting care of an eighteenth-century iron furnace at Duddon, in the southern part of the Park. Abandoned for over 100 years, the furnace is nevertheless in a good state of preservation and is one of the best examples in the country. The furnace was one of eight which nearly 300 years ago, used charcoal from local woodlands to smelt iron ore.

The National Parks have the planning system at their disposal, not only to influence the fate of old buildings, but also to control the appearance and location of new ones. Stricter planning rules apply in National Parks than in the rest of the country—for example, planning permission for a wider range of developments is needed, and some Parks produce their own design guides which have helped to influence the built environment for the better. On the other hand, excessive tweeness can sometimes be the result of too much conformity. Villages evolved over time, they did not suddenly emerge from a medieval or Victorian manual of good architectural practice. The challenge is to maintain the Parks' variety of regional styles while adventurously pursuing this diversity in new buildings.

But if the Parks insist on high standards of design and quality, will that mean that only the rich will be able to afford to build a house in a National Park? And if so, where will the locals live? Will they have to move away or will the Parks have to lower their standards?

Experience suggests that housing associations, or some similar collective enterprise, can best create new housing developments at prices which people can afford and to standards which everyone can applaud. But the Lake District and other authorities have found that it is not easy to devise methods of allocating houses strictly for the local population. And the Government has been no help.

Interior of Black Middens bastle barn, Northumberland, restored by English Heritage. Bastle barns were fortified to keep out marauders in the days of cross border raids.

Villages in the National Parks cannot be allowed to become mere collections of holiday homes, empty for half the year.

A desire for good standards of design, though laudable, can result in an excessive tweeness: these cottages in Bellingham, Northumberland, have an uncontrived charm.

Housesteads Fort, Hadrian's Wall.

Can National Parks survive their success?

AN ESCAPE OR AN INVASION?

*A National Park is no place
for time share developments
which bring with them
the paraphernalia of suburbia.*

*It is no place
for instant villages,
or for any developer
who is inspired by greed and whose developments
are characterised by poor taste.*

*To protect the National Parks
in order to enhance their beauty
is not a kill joy exercise,
a matter always of saying 'don't do that.'
It is a matter of saying:
'Don't do that, do this instead.
It will be better.'*

*The National Parks must be seen
not as places where
nasty things are not allowed to happen,
but as places where good things happen.*

I am a resident.
You are a holiday maker.
He is a tourist.

The snobbery is familiar. Tourism is, or was, a dirty word. Holidays are an escape, but tourism, too often, is seen as an invasion. And yet tourism can be a good thing. It can be good for an economy, because it brings in money, good for an environment, because the place has to be looking its best and good for people because it makes them happy.

But, it has to be managed.

The 1949 Act says precisely why National Parks were set up: '... for the purpose of preserving and enhancing the natural beauty (of the Parks) ... and for the purpose of promoting their enjoyment by the public.' Subsequent pronouncements by government have reinforced the Act with a rule that in the event of a conflict, the conservation of natural beauty comes first.

The question always to be asked is: does something protect or enhance the National Parks? Can people in large numbers enjoy the Parks and still protect and enhance their beauty?

The founders of the National Parks had little inkling of the rapid change to come, how incomes and car ownership would grow, and with them people's ability to get about. The early enthusiasts came on foot. The millions come by car.

If the Parks are to survive it will be necessary on occasion to say: 'No, that cannot be allowed.' This is neither to deny people their fundamental liberties, nor to spoil their enjoyment. It is a matter of discouraging people from doing things which disfigure the Parks, and of encouraging them to behave in a manner which ensures that there is still a Park to enjoy.

Cockshoot Broad in the Norfolk Broads was once foul with phosphates and fertilizer from adjoining farmland, its wildlife moribund and depleted. No one wanted to go there. Then the Broads Authority stepped in and cleaned the Broad. Clean water brought back the wildlife, and suddenly there was plenty to see. Once again Cockshoot was an inland lake fringed with reeds rich with wild creatures. The public returned and with them worries that the very success of the Broad would be its undoing. Nature-lovers feared that people would drive the wildlife away. The Broads Authority came up with a solution. They said no and yes at the same time. They built a hide from which everyone could see and enjoy the Broad, without disturbing the wildlife. Thousands of people have since marvelled at the secret life of Cockshoot Broad. It is better to have a peep than to have nothing to peep at.

In Pembrokeshire Coast National Park there is a village called Dale at the mouth of a little valley, which is ideal for launching a few boats or for strolling along the secluded beach. During the summer, it is choc-a-block with visitors, cars and boats. A car park is proposed to relieve the congestion caused by informal roadside parking and an old meadow a few yards from the beach is tarmaced for the purpose. No sooner is it in operation than it is soon full and cars are once again spilling onto the narrow road, causing congestion. Another car park is suggested, and a wider road, which in turn would bring more cars and another car park . . .

It was not allowed to happen. Why should local people suffer ever more cars, wider roads and a rash of car parks which are empty for forty weeks of the year? Can the spread of car parks be considered to protect or enhance the Park? If a field under tarmac was an old water meadow, it cannot be recreated if the car park becomes redundant. Should not some parts of the National Parks be left alone, to be discovered just as they are? And if so, how?

Different Parks have offered different answers. They have offered restricted parking to those who cannot walk far, such as disabled people. They have said no to other people and asked them to leave their cars outside the valley, on a piece of derelict or disused land, where providing a car park is less intrusive. If the distance is not far, people have been asked to walk, or a special bus service has been provided.

'Park and ride' and other transport schemes have been extremely successful in National Parks. In the Lake District, the Mountain Goat is heavily used to show visitors the sights and to pick up walkers returning from the fells. In Northumberland, the Park Authority supports a bus service which drops visitors off at sites along Hadrian's Wall.

In National Parks combining public transport with people's own car travel has an important part to play in protecting the Parks, and the transport services are a boon to the local communities. The problem as always is lack of money. The Peak Park had to abandon its bus service when a special grant ran out.

In all National Parks there are centres where shops, souvenirs, hotels and pubs abound. Countryside planners have coined the word 'honeypots' to describe them. Honeypots are busy, bustling, crowded, and in season, frequently congested. They take some of the pressure off other parts of the Parks, but do little or nothing to protect or enhance the National Parks. Bowness-on-Windermere is one example of a honeypot gone mad; even the visitors say it is too commercialised and overcrowded.

Some planners would redraw the National Park bound-

Swaledale souvenirs, woollens on sale at Muker, Yorkshire Dales.

aries to exclude the honeypots, just as the original boundary of the Peak Park was drawn to exclude Buxton and the quarries around it. But that is the coward's way out. Better to learn the lessons of the honeypots and determine both to correct the errors and not to repeat them.

The most difficult decision Park Authorities face is to say 'No' to new developments which have a spurious attraction but which are wholly out of place in a National Park. There is a new breed of developers seeking to make millions out of the National Parks, developers whose schemes are set to transform the Parks into creeping suburbia, developers who have covetous eyes on some of the Parks most beautiful, and least spoilt, countryside. The stakes are high.

In the Lake District, where leisure complexes and time share already spawn, a developer plans to turn a former caravan site into a 74-unit time-share complex, together with 98 holiday cottages, 60 serviced apartments, 133 caravans, restaurants, a private marina and a leisure centre. All this is on the shores of Windermere.

In the Brecon Beacons, to which developers are now turning their attention, 240 prefabricated mock Tudor time share cottages are set to cover 130 acres of the banks of the lovely River Usk, under the lea of the Black Mountains—along with a 'central leisure complex' linked by walkways, with underground parking for 150 cars, overground parking for 160 cars, solarium, gym, sauna, squash courts, and a banqueting hall.

Should that be allowed in a National Park?

Developers of such schemes argue their case on the basis of 'planning gain', 'improving a scruffy site, or removing an eyesore. They say that by adhering to good design standards and by using some local materials their developments are in keeping with the National Park. They claim that hundreds of local jobs will be created. They promise facilities for use by local communities throughout the year.

But these are developments on a very large scale. They may start life as modest time share accommodation but then pieces are added. Applications are submitted for the 'add-ons'—the leisure centre, the sauna, the solarium, the restaurants and the staff accommodation. It is the add-ons which make the real money, which separate the visitors from their holiday cash, and increasingly the add-ons are central to the whole enterprise.

These new developments are intended for car owners, so car parks are essential, and they are intended to be used throughout the year. No amount of screening and local building materials can make this tourism on a mass scale fit for a National Park. It neither protects nor enhances, and it spoils other people's enjoyment.

It may be all right on the edge of a city or in an inner city, but not in a National Park.

You don't go to the Lake District to pump iron in a gym and blow dry your hair in the changing room. The Lakes themselves are the attraction, and if enjoying the scenery means changing the countryside, something is wrong. And it cannot be allowed to happen.

Expensive time share also puts a price on public enjoyment of the National Parks. A wonderful view from the top floor of your £9,000 a week luxury time share cottage in its leisure centre setting means someone else's pleasure in unspoilt natural beauty is ruined. A five-star holiday village taking up 100 acres of land means having to pay for the privilege of walking by the lakeside, or walking somewhere else. National Parks then become available only to those who can afford them.

The Langdale time share complex in the Lake District, which opened in 1982, marked a new era in leisure developments in National Parks. The 23-acre complex, formerly the site of a gunpowder works, includes 77 self-catering 'Norwegian style' time share lodges, a sports and leisure centre with a swimming pool offering a 'Caribbean-beach type environment' and a major face-lift for the Pillar Hotel.

Langdale is not an eyesore: it could even be presented as an 'environmental improvement' of a run down site. But it represents a scale of commercial activity which threatens the quiet sanctuary of the National Parks.

Journalist Colin Speakman, writing in The Great Outdoors puts it well: 'It seems quiet enjoyment of the uniquely beautiful landscape is no longer sufficient for the modern tourist industry, which must bring the artificial entertainments and sophisticated paraphernalia of modern urban life to destroy that very solitude and natural beauty National Parks were intended to preserve.
'Such developments could pose the gravest challenge yet experienced to the integrity of the Lake District, and, in due course, to other great landscapes as the leisure boom gets underway.'

Profits generated by such ventures frequently go outside the Parks to the consortia of international leisure companies which increasingly own them. And these profits are made at the expense of low key, local businesses whose livelihood depends upon visitors coming to enjoy unspoilt natural beauty. Recent research shows that "uncommercialised" countryside is the major attraction of a National Park.

What about jobs? Developers like to make optimistic estimates of their powers of job creation. The reality often falls short of the rhetoric. The jobs themselves are predominantly part time, seasonal and low paid. Leisure companies usually bring in their own management from outside so there are not many career opportunities for local people.

National Park Authorities cannot ignore the need for employment. It concerns them deeply. The law says they must have regard to it in their policies, and they do. Their task is to encourage and promote the right kind of economic activity, the kind which protects and enhances the Parks. There is much work to be done—all of it gainful employment.

In the pubs in the Lake District local people are not talking about all these new leisure jobs, but about what time share and the holiday cottage is doing to house prices. They resent sites with planning permission going to build time share villages and not to homes for local people. They wonder how their children will ever be able to afford to live in the Lakes. The full time occupants of a National Park, who work in it or nearby, find the problem of accommodation almost insuperable. A few years ago the Lake District Board tried to introduce a new planning rule which restricted some homes to local ownership, but the Government would have none of it.

Whatever the Parks decide, they are on trial by public jury and by the local press. And sometimes local councillors on the Park boards or committees see things purely in local terms and forget that they act as stewards of a national inheritance. To stand back, to take a strategic and national view of what is happening, to say that the development in question does not belong in the National Park, to infer that the cumulative effect of what is happening means having to say stop before it is too late, takes a lot of courage and a belief in the integrity of the National Parks.

To their credit the Parks mostly try to do the right thing—only to have the Government impose its own wishes when a developer has appealed against the Park's decision. In the Lake District, so many decisions have been overturned that the Park has complained directly to the minister. Such undermining of the Parks' decisions hardly inspires them with confidence. But it is not an exaggeration to say that unless checked, large-scale leisure developments could irrevocably change the face of the National Parks. It is as serious as that.

A cabin-cruiser being laid up for the winter in the Norfolk Broads. Boating is one of the best ways to enjoy the Broads. But without control of numbers and pollution, cruisers could threaten the beauty of the waterways. Traditional sail and paddle power offer a pollution-free alternative.

Quarrying at Cracoe, Yorkshire Dales.

IN WHOSE
NATIONAL INTEREST?

The Parks must come first.
Wherever competing interests conflict
the Parks are the priority.
And there are many threats
to their integrity.

What is quarrying
but the authorised removal of a Park?
Once you have dug out a chunk,
you cannot say that you are sorry
and that you will put it back again.
There should be no question of quarrying in the Parks
for minerals that can be found elsewhere

A National Park is no place
for permanent military manoeuvres,
for exercises with live ammunition,
for the requisition of beautiful acres
from which the public
is then excluded.
It is no place
for low flying military aircraft
shattering the silence of the dales.

'Who', said a Government Inspector as he looked down on a new development in the Lake District, 'gave permission for that monstrosity?'

'You did,' came the reply.

It is a story often repeated in the Lakes and it is not a joke.

National Park Authorities endeavour to balance the needs and interests of local communities with the national interest with which they are entrusted: the protection and enhancement of beautiful countryside for public enjoyment.

However, the government's idea of the 'national interest' appears to override anyone else's 'national interest', and National Parks have been poorly served over the years by governments of all political persuasions. While the Parks have been able to prevent the small man doing the small thing, their attempts to prevent the large developer and his large-scale development have been squashed by government again and again.

'Where a government department has had plans for erecting large installations of one kind or another in a national park, I can remember no case where it has been diverted from its purpose by anything that the Commission might say . . .'—So said Lord Strang, head of the National Parks Commission (now the Countryside Commission) in 1962. Nothing changes.

The 1980s have merely continued the trend of indifference, even of opposition, towards National Parks by Government departments. In 1980, the Department of the Environment allowed ICI to extend its Tunstead Quarry on the edge of the Peak District, against the wishes of the Park Authority. In 1985, the Department of Transport overturned a decision by a committee of the Houses of Parliament to route the Okehampton bypass outside the

Dartmoor National Park. Instead the bypass has been driven through it, destroying a medieval deer park, just to save a few acres of farmland, which in the new farming climate, could well go out of production anyway.

The Okehampton bypass under construction in the Dartmoor National Park. The bypass has obliterated an ancient medieval deerpark—with the blessing of the Department of Transport.

In 1987 the Government decided to build a new Anti-Ballistic Missile Warning System at Fylingdales in the North York Moors National Park.

The Ministry of Defence is the most indifferent of all to the National Parks. It points out that the military—which now occupy large areas of Dartmoor and Northumberland and parts of the Pembrokeshire coastline—were there first, which is true. But on a ticket marked 'national security', the military not only seem to be parked permanently on some of the best bits of the Parks, but, in an entirely unaccountable fashion, do more or less what they want.

Live firing and people do not mix, which is why live firing should not be permitted in the National Parks. Not only is public access to military training land barred on training days, but in some areas, this means permanently throughout the year. On Dartmoor, the army has stopped notifying people in some of the local post offices of its firing days when the ranges will be out of bounds. Faced with a map with danger in red all over it, and no specific information except through the local papers, the effect is a permanent deterrent to anyone seeking the solitude and beauty of the moors.

Military occupation in Northumberland. The presence of the military means in National Parks huge areas of land are barred from public access, in some cases permanently throughout the year. In Northumberland, 22 per cent of the land is used for military training. As yet there has been no serious attempt by the Ministry of Defence to seek alternative training areas outside the Parks.

DANGER
MINISTRY OF DEFENCE RANGE
THE GENERAL PUBLIC MUST NOT PASS
THIS POINT WHILE RED FLAGS ARE FLYING
OR LAMPS ARE DISPLAYED
ADMITTANCE TO AUTHORISED
PERSONS ONLY

Even if the army is absent it can still be dangerous. In 1987, a young boy picked up an unexploded shell on Dartmoor and nearly blew himself to smithereens. Fortunately he was not killed, but he was very seriously injured. In the Pembrokeshire Coast, the Castle Martin ranges are out of bounds because there is said to be live ammunition lying around after training. But during the winter, local farmers come on to the ranges with their sheep, and no one has yet been blown up. Except for a few guided walks organised by the National Parks, access there means an eight-mile detour inland for anyone on the long-distance coastal path and a beautiful beach barred to the public.

The Ministry of Defence has made much of the fact that its training areas have become nature reserves rich in wildlife. What the Ministry prefers not to explain is that this has happened because its land has escaped intensive agriculture and forestry, not because its land is undisturbed by people. It would be nice to be allowed a glimpse of the wildlife.

What most offends about the military presence in the National Parks is the unaccountability. There is no serious attempt to justify the presence, no search for alternative sites, no thought that National Parks should be the last place for such activities. The army is becoming entrenched and on Dartmoor is seeking to build a new permanent camp to accommodate soldiers training on its live-firing ranges. The armed forces must indeed be trained but must they fire live ammunition in the most beautiful parts of the land? If there is no alternative, so be it, but no one has yet looked.

If National Parks are not pounded by guns, they are under attack from quarry blasting. In whose interest is it that limestone is gouged from hillsides, leaving behind ugly scars? Can it be right that limestone which goes to make roads is extracted from the most beautiful parts of the country? There are many other quarries not in National Parks where roadstone can be obtained.

There is a test governments are supposed to apply when considering quarrying in National Parks. It was most recently clarified in a statement in Parliament in 1987. The test is quite clear and can be determined by considering the following questions. Is there a national need for the mineral? What will be the effect on the local economy of saying yes or no to extraction? Can an alternative be found somewhere else? Will quarrying have a detrimental effect on the landscape? And, weighing all this up, will the development be in the public interest? Not a bad mechanism for making the all important decision, where National Parks have a fair chance of winning—if only it were rigorously applied.

Local, traditional quarrying has never been a worry. It is traditional in the sense that the operation is small-scale and it is labour intensive. But now machines hew out hillsides at a greater rate with only a handful of men, and that is no longer traditional quarrying.

In the Lake District, an application to extend the Elterwater slate quarry was turned down by the Park. But local pressure forced the Board to change its mind. Many jobs would be lost and a local industry supplying local needs destroyed, it was said. In fact much of the slate goes for export to furnish mantlepieces for millionaires in Minnesota and the jobs claim is exaggerated. And to return to the fundamental question, does the activity enhance or protect the Park? Quarrying on a large scale does not.

But people in the Parks must have work. Ideally the work should be found in the very activity of protecting and enhancing the Parks, in managing them and looking after them. A great workforce is needed for every task from

Quarrying leaves a permanent scar on the landscape, as this quarrying operation near Buxton in the Peak Park (right) shows. The screen of conifers fails to hide the damage of the quarrying at Biddestone (above) in the Northumberland National Park. Is such destruction of the National Parks in the national interest?

dry-stone walling to woodland care.

And there can be hi-tech jobs too. In the Peak Park, Microplants, a company which produces plants by a new technology, is comfortably established in a traditional stone building.

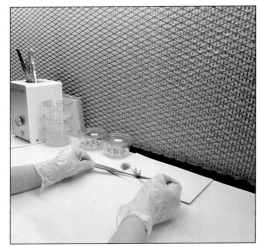

People in National Parks must have work. Tucked away inside a traditional building in the Peak Park, the high-tech interior of Microplants demonstrates that clean, small-scale businesses, sited in the right place, can provide jobs without spoiling the environment.

Another Park-based business, jeweller C.W. Sellors, has its own workshop which provides jobs for young people.

A computer company which planned to move to Bakewell would have been welcome in the Park—on the right site. Unfortunately the Development Commission which encouraged the move, did not talk to the National Park first, and foolishly suggested that the company should set up on a green field site in an area of prime beauty, strictly against the Park's planning guidelines. The Park offered the company another site where development would be welcome and not a threat.

The national interest of natural beauty and public enjoyment invested in the Park Authorities is also the local interest. The Daugleddau in the Pembrokeshire Coast National Park is a wide and tranquil estuary, the confluence of several rivers, where old meadows come down to meet the water and the seabass jump in the tidal eddies. The Park is developing an 80-mile circular ramble around the estuary, with just enough promotion to tell people about it, fully intending that the area should remain remote and secluded, one of the Park's quieter sanctuaries.

Yet walkers passing through villages and small towns will spend money in local shops, pubs and bed and breakfast. They may drop in to the Lawrenny workshops, where small-scale industries have been encouraged in low-cost accommodation. They may take the ferry boat from one side of the estuary to the other. Local people will benefit. So will the Park. Government departments are beginning to realise this.

In 1986, the Government dismissed an appeal by a quarry company to extend a quarry at Topley Pike in the Peak District, and again at Eldon Hill in 1987. In the same year, the Council for National Parks successfully persuaded the Central Electricity Generating Board not to quarry limestone from National Parks, to clean up its power stations. In 1988, the government refused an appeal by

Mercury Communications to build a telecommunications tower on Beacon Hill in the North York Moors National Park, after strong opposition from the Park, its supporters, and the Council for National Parks.

So it can be done, not by seeking compromise, but by re-stating the principles of the National Parks. Protect and enhance, or be off.

Protecting the National Parks means protecting the livelihoods of local people. Visitors come to the Parks to enjoy natural beauty. They spend money in local shops. David May's Village Store in the Yorkshire Dales also acts as an information point for the Park.

Sunset over Parley Common, New Forest.

The oil refinery in the Pembrokeshire Coast National Park (opposite) is due to close by the end of the century. Will the coastline be restored or will a new industry take its place?

A FUTURE FOR
NATIONAL PARKS

*What is needed is
for the National Park Authorities
to have the powers
and the money,
and the understanding,
so that they can fulfil
their obligation to their inheritance.*

There are ten National Parks in England and Wales but there ought to be more. The Broads is now a National Park in all but name, although the legislation bringing this into effect is ill-phrased. It fails to make it clear that the Broads must come first if there is any conflict of interests.

The New Forest, perhaps the most threatened beautiful place of all in England, needs greater protection, and there are parts of the North of England and Wales, including the North Pennines and the Northumberland coast, which should be embraced while there is still time.

North of the Border there are those who argue that Scotland is a National Park and there are those who want none of it. Many country lovers in Scotland fear that too much regulation will restrict their freedom in a country where the pressure of population is as nothing, say, with the Peak District. But as the tree-planting tax-avoiding antics have demonstrated, there are real threats to the Scottish countryside. What is certain is that Scotland will want to find its own solution and not have something imposed upon it.

But in England and Wales the National Park is the best idea anyone has come up with yet to look after the most beautiful parts of the countryside. Without the Parks, many much-loved landscapes would have been lost. Villages would have become towns. Towns would have sprawled. The pace of change would have been faster. Fewer battles would have been won. Worse still, the battles may not have been fought at all. That is why the Parks should command the support of everyone who cares about the countryside.

It is too easy to approve of National Parks in principle while allowing them to be tampered with in practice. Inquiries are conducted and appeals allowed on development proposals which should have been dismissed as wholly out of place in a National Park.

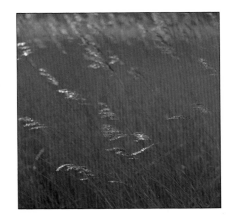

The Broads must come first.

The New Forest is perhaps the most threatened beautiful place in England. It is a remarkable piece of living history, a reminder of how the countryside looked in the days of William the Conqueror. Its ancient heaths and woodlands, which have been grazed by animals for centuries, support some of the richest wildlife in Europe.

A mighty Forest Beech

A typical New Forest barn

Gravestones at the parish church of All Saints, Minstead

Ponies grazing the open heaths of the New Forest. Animals are vital to the survival of the Forest. Their grazing helps to maintain its open character.

Most of the New Forest is owned by the Crown – but this is not enough to keep the threats at bay. The next decade will see increasing pressure on the Forest from oil exploration, roads and suburban development. Many people believe that the Forest needs statutory protection before it is too late. Should it become the next member of the National Park family?

But even more important is to encourage appropriate developments in National Parks, to set an example. It is so much easier to reject a bad idea when you have a better one to put in its place.

National Parks are essential and exciting testbeds for new ways of doing things; new ways of looking after the countryside and new ways of ensuring the livelihoods of rural communities. The Parks are doing pioneering work to help farmers tend their land in a way which protects and enhances the landscape. The Parks are encouraging new businesses which are in harmony with their surroundings, in a lasting relationship where both benefit. The Parks are showing the way forward for economies based on balance not exploitation. The sort of economies arising out of the new computer technologies. The Parks are not an exercise in rural nostalgia, seeking to preserve an old order against all odds.

Yet National Parks could work so much better. They need a greater degree of independence and a better mix of local and national interests in their administration. They need more money, not simply because they have so little, not simply because there is always more work to do than there is money available, but because of the contribution they can make to the wider countryside. National Parks are an investment for the whole country.

Future generations
will have inventions which
we cannot even dream of,
but with our help they will also have
the National Parks
that we know and love.

*National Parks arose out of the desire of people to escape the
grime of the cities. Danby Station in the North York Moors
is still a welcome sight to the city weary.*

National Parks will always be special, but they do not sit in splendid isolation. To support the National Parks should never mean that the rest of the countryside does not matter in its own right. It does.

Is there a future for places like this?

With your help there can be.

The Council for National Parks is the charity which fights to keep National Parks beautiful for you to enjoy. If you would like to support this work become a Friend of National Parks.

As a Friend of National Parks you get:

- Our magazine *Tarn & Tor* three times a year, full of the latest National Parks news and views

- The colour magazine *National Parks Today* three times a year

- Free guided walks in National Parks

- Special events for Friends throughout the year

- Discounts on National Park publications

To become a Friend, please fill in the form below and return it to the Friends Secretary, Council for National Parks, 45 Shelton Street, London WC2H 9HJ, or telephone 01 240 3603.
Cheques should be made payable to the
Council for National Parks.

I would like to become a Friend of National Parks:

Single £7.50 Joint £10, Life £150 (Single) Life £200 (Joint)

NAME

ADDRESS

I enclose cheque for £

National Park Fund

Donations to the National Park Fund are used directly to secure the future of our Parks for you to enjoy. Projects for which money from the Fund is available include

- buying land to ensure that its management is in safe hands

- research – to find solutions to Park problems

- fighting major threats

- helping local organisations working in the Parks

- expanding the Council's range of activities.

If you wish to make a donation to the National Park Fund please send a cheque made payable to the National Park Fund to: Diane Bell, Council for National Parks, 45 Shelton Street, London WC2H 9HJ.

Reg. Charity No. 295336

SELECTED BIBLIOGRAPHY

COUNCIL FOR NATIONAL PARKS, *Fifty years for National Parks*, 1986

COUNTRYSIDE COMMISSION, Individual guides to the 10 National Parks, Webb & Bower

MACEWAN, ANN AND MALCOLM, *Green Prints for the Countryside*, Allen & Unwin, 1987

MACEWAN, ANN AND MALCOLM, *National Parks: Conservation or Cosmetics*, George Allen and Unwin, 1982

INFORMATION

Brecon Beacons National Park
7 Glamorgan Street, Brecon, Powys LD3 7DP.
Tel: 0874 4437.

Dartmoor National Park
Parke, Haytor Road, Bovey Tracey, Devon
TQ13 9JQ. Tel: 0620 832093.

Exmoor National Park
Exmoor House, Dulverton, Somerset TA22
9HL. Tel: 0398 23665.

Lake District National Park
National Park Visitor Centre, Brockhole, Windermere, Cumbria LA23 1LJ. Tel: 09662 6601.

Norfolk and Suffolk Broads
The Broads Authority, Thomas Harvey House,
18 Colgate, Norwich NR3 1BQ.

Northumberland National Park
Eastburn, South Park, Hexham, Northumberland NE46 1BS. Tel: 0434 605555.

North York Moors National Park
The Old Vicarage, Bondgate, Helmsley, York
YO6 5BP. Tel: 0439 70657.

Peak District National Park
Aldern House, Baslow Road, Bakewell, Derbyshire DE4 1AE. 062 981 4321.

Pembrokeshire Coast National Park
County Offices, Haverfordwest, Dyfed SA61
1QZ. Tel: 0437 4591.

Snowdonia National Park
Penrhyndeudraeth, Gwynedd LL48 6LS. Tel:
0766 770274.

Yorkshire Dales National Park
Colvend, Hebden Road, Grassington, Skipton
BD23 5LB. Tel: 0756 752748.

The Council for National Parks would like to thank all its
Friends and allies for their help and support.